Reading Essentials® in Science

EARTH EXPLORATIONS II

W0006174

Mapping the Earth

TRACI STECKEL PEDERSEN

PERFECTION LEARNING®

Editorial Director: Susan C. Thies
Editor: Mary L. Bush
Design Director: Randy Messer
Book Design: Robin Elwick, Tobi Cunningham
Cover Design: Michael Aspengren

A special thanks to the following for his scientific review of the book:
Kristin Mandsager, Instructor of Physics and Astronomy,
Garden City Community College

Image Credits:
©Take 2 Productions/Ken Kaminesky/CORBIS: p. 4 (bottom); ©Michael Nicholson/CORBIS: p. 9;
©Bettmann/CORBIS: pp. 10, 11; ©Gianni Dagli Orti/CORBIS: p. 12 (top); ©Archivo Iconografico, S.A./
CORBIS: p. 13; ©Roger Ressmeyer/CORBIS: p. 36

Corbis Royalty-Free: front cover; istockphoto.com: back cover, pp. 3, 4 (top), 6, 7 (bottom),
12 (bottom), 14, 15, 19 (bottom), 21, 24, 25, 26, 27 (bottom), 28, 34 (top), 35 (bottom), 39, 40;
photos.com: pp. 1, 5, 7 (top), 16–17 (background), 22, 27 (top), 34 (bottom); Perfection Learning:
pp. 8, 16, 17, 23, 31, 35 (top); Courtesy of the University of Texas Libraries, The University of Texas
at Austin: p. 18; Library of Congress, Geography and Map Division: pp. 32, 33; National Oceanic
and Atmospheric Administration/NOAA: pp. 29, 30; Map Resources: p. 20

For information, contact
Perfection Learning® Corporation
1000 North Second Avenue, P.O. Box 500
Logan, Iowa 51546-0500.
Phone: 1-800-831-4190
Fax: 1-800-543-2745
perfectionlearning.com

1 2 3 4 5 6 PP 11 10 09 08 07 06

PB ISBN 0-7891-7017-5
RLB ISBN 0-7569-6652-3

Table of Contents

1. Virtual and Real-Life Representation . . . 4

2. Mapping the Past 7

3. The Mapmaker's Tools 14

4. Round Earth, Flat Paper 22

5. Many Scientific Maps 27

6. Mapping Technology 34

Internet Connections and
Related Reading for Maps 37

Glossary 38

Index 40

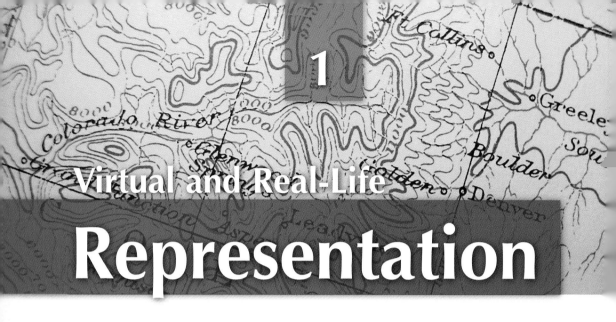

1

Virtual and Real-Life
Representation

In many of today's video games, navigation is the key to survival. Entire worlds are built around the characters, and you are the guide. The **map** in the corner of the screen becomes one of your most valuable tools as you navigate characters through tunnels, castles, caves, or cities. Without the map, you'd have no way of knowing which direction to go or how to get from one point to the other. You'd be trapped in a virtual maze of confusion.

Maps also help you navigate your way in the real world. They can tell you which direction you should turn to reach a destination. They can tell you where to find mountains for hiking or rivers for canoeing. They can even tell you what the weather will be like when you arrive.

So What *Is* a Map?

What comes to mind when you think of a map? The road map that you keep in your car or the globe that sits in your classroom? These items are what most people think of when they hear the word *map*. But there are actually many other types of maps. There are maps of the ocean floor, maps that show the location of natural resources, and maps that show where earthquakes are likely to occur. There are also maps that show the weather patterns and **biomes** around the world.

What do all of these maps have in common? They are representations, or models, of features found on all or part of the Earth's surface. Road maps show the streets and highways in a certain location. Ocean floor maps show landforms at the bottom of the ocean. **Climate** maps show the weather elements in an area. Every map is designed to present some kind of information about the Earth in a visual manner.

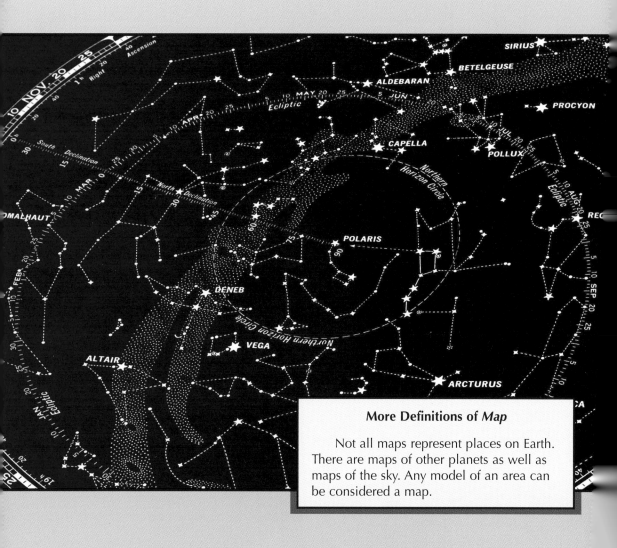

SIRIUS

BETELGEUSE

ALDEBARAN

PROCYON

CAPELLA

POLLUX

Ecliptic

Northern Horizon Circle

POLARIS

REC

OMALHAUT

North Declination

South Declination

Right Ascension

Ecliptic

DENEB

Northern Horizon Circle

VEGA

ALTAIR

ARCTURUS

More Definitions of *Map*

Not all maps represent places on Earth. There are maps of other planets as well as maps of the sky. Any model of an area can be considered a map.

The Science of Mapmaking

Cartography is the science of mapmaking. Because the world and our knowledge of it are constantly changing, cartographers have the important task of making new maps to reflect these changes.

2

Mapping the Past

Treasure maps have long been associated with pirates and buried gold. And while most of these tales are exaggerated, the mystery and excitement surrounding historical maps remains.

Scientists who study old maps look at every detail, from the locations pinpointed to the materials used to create the maps. Each piece of information reveals clues about the culture and time period the map belonged to. These historical maps help us discover what the world was like long ago—or at least what people *thought* the world was like.

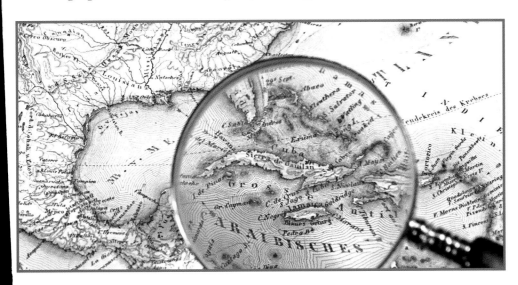

Map Materials

Maps have always been created with whatever materials were available. In the beginning of mapmaking, this may have been a finger moving around in the dirt or sand. Evidence shows that early Eskimos sketched locations or directions on ivory, sand, or animal skins. People living in the Marshall Islands of the Pacific wove sticks and fibers together to represent ocean currents and wave patterns. They even used little shells to mark the islands.

The oldest surviving "world" map was made in Babylonia (now Iraq) more than 2500 years ago. A Babylonian mapmaker used a sharp object to carve the map into clay. This ancient clay map features Babylonia in the center with Assyria and Chaldea on either side. Mountains border the kingdom to the north, and water surrounds all the land.

As civilizations advanced, so did the mapmaking materials. The Egyptians used papyrus, an early form of paper. Europeans used parchment made from the skins of sheep or goats. Silk was the map material of choice for the Chinese. And by the 1500s, maps were made from copper or steel engravings.

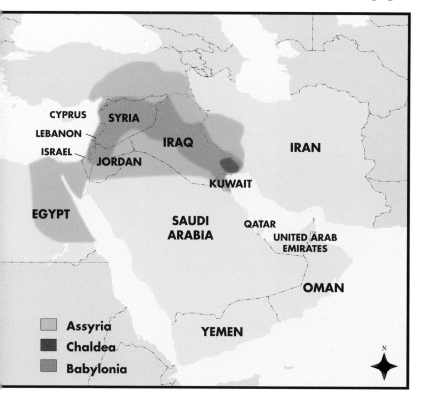

A modern-day map of the Middle East showing the former locations of Assyria, Chaldea, and Babylonia

The First Book of Maps

The first book of maps was made by Ptolemy (TAHL uh mee), an astronomer and geographer in the middle of the 2nd century A.D. Like other Greek philosophers and scientists, Ptolemy believed the Earth was a sphere, not flat like most people thought. In his book *Geographia*, Ptolemy wrote instructions on how to draw a round Earth on a flat piece of paper. He also used **latitude** and **longitude** to locate about 8000 places that were known to exist.

A re-creation of Ptolemy's map

Ptolemy's world map featured three continents—Europe, Asia, and Africa. The continents were not represented correctly, but Ptolemy drew them to the best of his and other scientists' knowledge at the time. Asia, for example, stretched too far east and China was way too big. Africa stretched southward and connected with Terra Australis Incognita, the unknown land of the South. (Ptolemy and many others believed that there must be a large "unknown" continent south of the equator to balance out all the continents above it.) Even with these mistakes, Ptolemy's book contained advanced ideas about mapmaking that were respected for a long time.

Scientist of Significance

In 1540, a German cartographer and cosmographer named Sebastian Munster revised Ptolemy's *Geographia* using updated information about the New World. Munster's maps were far more accurate than all previous world maps. On Munster's maps, North and South America were connected to each other and completely separated from Asia. The new edition of *Geographia* became an extremely influential book in the field of cartography.

In 1544, Munster published his own book called *Cosmographia*. **Cosmography** is the study of mapping the entire world or universe. *Cosmographia* was the first description of the world from the German point of view. The book was published in several different languages and became popular in many countries. It helped motivate others to pursue mapmaking.

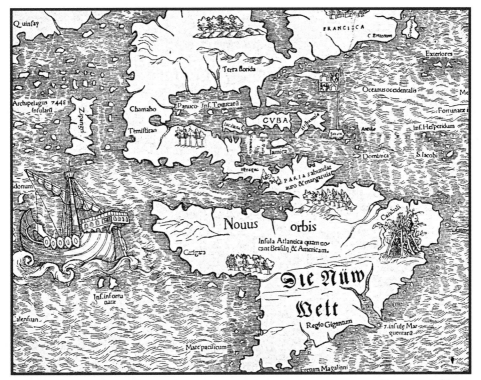

Engraving from Munster's *Cosmographia*

Medieval Maps

In the Middle Ages (5th century to 15th century), religion played a large role in society. This had a great influence on mapmaking. Religious sites were popular center points on medieval maps. The Psalter Map, created about 1225, features Jerusalem at its center and includes the Dead Sea, the city of Jericho, and other lands featured in the *Bible*.

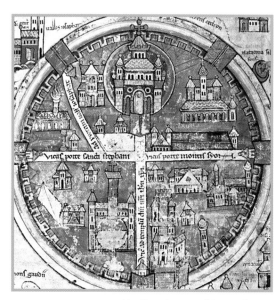

Medieval map of Jerusalem

Sea charts, or portolan maps, were also created toward the end of the Middle Ages. These charts were used by sailors as they made their way across the ocean. Sea charts showed bodies of water, coastlines, and ports. Many also labeled ocean currents, wind directions, and sailing distances.

Tracing the Path of Science

Although Ptolemy placed north at the top of his maps, medieval maps did not follow this guide. On medieval maps, north was on the left side of the map and east was at the top. This finally changed when sailors began placing their compasses on top of sea charts to help them navigate. Because the magnetic needle on the compass always pointed north, the direction of north on maps was moved to the top. It is still found here today on the majority of maps.

The First Atlas

Soon after the invention of the printing press in the mid-1400s, mapmaking became a big business, and nobody sold more maps than the Dutch. In fact, the time period from 1550 to 1675 is referred to as the Golden Age of Dutch Cartography. During this time, the Dutch became experts at drawing, painting, and printing maps.

In 1570, a Dutch mapmaker named Abraham Ortelius published the *Theatrum Orbis Terrarum* (*The Theater of the World*). This book of maps is considered the first modern **atlas** and was the most expensive book on the market at the time. It set the standard for the many atlases that were to follow.

Mapping the World

The next several centuries were a period of exploration and discovery. Territories were purchased, countries were established, and states were formed. Each change was a new opportunity for mapmakers who strived to create accurate representations of cities, states, countries, and continents. Even today, mapmakers must meet the challenge of keeping up with an ever-changing world.

3

The Mapmaker's Tools

Although maps have varied throughout history, certain features began to appear again and again and became consistent elements of maps. These mapping "tools" enable everyone to read and understand a variety of maps.

Getting the Directions

The **compass rose** was first developed and used on medieval sea charts. Sailors originally used the North Star and magnetic compasses to guide their trips. So when they made maps of the oceans, they recognized the importance of knowing directions and included a compass on their maps.

A compass rose is the illustration on a map that indicates directions. It is called a compass "rose" because the star shape in the center looks like a flower. Each of the "petals" points in a certain direction.

Some maps have simpler compasses. There may be just a cross with the directions indicated on it or a single arrow indicating which way is north. The style of the compass doesn't matter as long as it shows in which direction the map is oriented.

15

Inquire and Investigate
Compasses

Question: Does the needle on a compass need to be magnetized in order to always point north?

Answer the question: I think the needle on a compass _____.

Form a hypothesis: The needle on a compass (does/does not) need to be magnetized in order to always point north.

Test the hypothesis:

Materials
glass or plastic bowl (NOT metal)
water
slice of cork about ¼-inch thick
sewing needle
magnet

Procedure
- Determine which way is north, south, east, and west in your classroom.
- Fill the bowl about three-fourths full with water. Place the piece of cork in the water. It should float.
- Lay the needle on the cork and observe what happens. Which way does the needle point when it's settled? [Pay attention to which end of the needle you're considering the "pointer" (either the tip or the eye) and continue to observe that end of the needle.]
- Pick up the cork and turn it so the needle is facing a different direction. Put the cork back in the water and watch what happens. Repeat this procedure several times, recording your observations.

- Now magnetize the needle by rubbing it across the magnet in the same direction at least 30 times. Do *not* rub the needle back and forth on the magnet.
- Lay the magnetized needle on the cork and observe what happens. Which way does the needle point when it's settled? [Pay attention to which end of the needle (tip or eye) is pointing north and continue to observe that end of the needle.]
- Pick up the cork and turn it so the needle is facing a different direction. Put the cork back in the water and watch what happens. Repeat this procedure several times, recording your observations.

Observations: The unmagnetized needle points in the direction it was placed. For example, if it is placed in the water pointing west, then it remains pointing west. No matter which direction the magnetized needle is pointing when you set it down, it always turns so it's pointing north.

Conclusions: The needle on a compass does need to be magnetized in order to always point north. This is because the Earth's metallic core acts like a magnet, twisting other magnetic objects into alignment with its magnetic field lines. The geographic North Pole on Earth is actually a magnetic south pole, while the geographic South Pole is actually a magnetic north pole. So the north-seeking end of a magnet or magnetized object always points to geographic north (magnetic south) because magnetic opposites attract. This is how a compass works.

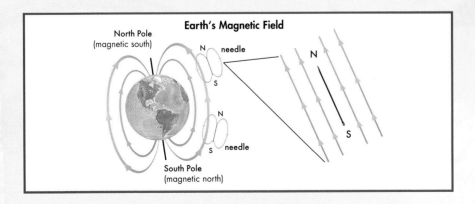

Earth's Magnetic Field

Scaling the Map

Obviously maps are not life-size. Instead they are drawn to a certain proportion of the real area. The **scale** on a map tells you how to figure out the actual size of the area shown on a map.

Scales come in various forms. Some are simply stated on the map. For instance, it may say "1 inch equals 100 miles." Other scales are written as ratios. For example, a ratio of 1:500,000 means that every 1 unit on the map is equal to 500,000 of those units in real life. So 1 inch on the map equals 500,000 inches in real life, and 1 centimeter on the map equals 500,000 centimeters in real life. Scales can also be shown graphically with a bar that shows how much a distance on the map represents in real life.

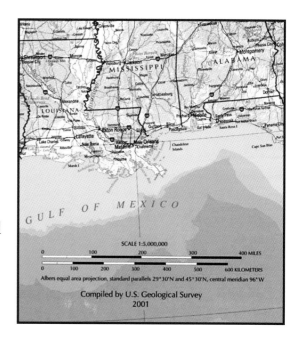

Maps can be classified as either large-scale or small-scale. A large-scale map shows a small area in great detail. City or neighborhood maps are examples of large-scale maps. A world map, on the other hand, is a small-scale map. A small-scale map shows a large area with less detail.

Large-scale map of Washington, D.C.

The Key to the Map

Symbols and colors are often used to represent things on maps. A symbol is a small picture that stands for something else. Common map symbols include lines for highways, stars within circles for capital cities, trees for forests, and triangles for mountains.

Mapmakers use color to highlight or separate features or areas. Color is often used to show countries, states, climates, elevations, or landforms.

How can you tell what a symbol or color stands for? Use the **key**, or **legend**. The key explains what all of the symbols or colors on a map represent.

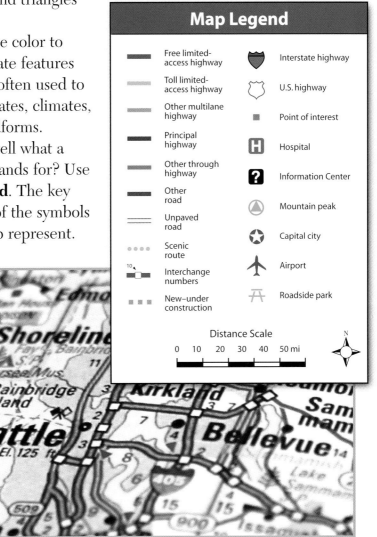

Map Legend

Free limited-access highway	Interstate highway
Toll limited-access highway	U.S. highway
Other multilane highway	Point of interest
Principal highway	H Hospital
Other through highway	? Information Center
Other road	Mountain peak
Unpaved road	Capital city
Scenic route	Airport
Interchange numbers	Roadside park
New—under construction	

Distance Scale

0   10   20   30   40   50 mi

N

Staying Inside the Lines

The lines circling the globe horizontally (east–west) are called *lines of latitude*. The line of latitude that divides the globe in half is the equator. The equator divides the Earth into the Northern and Southern Hemispheres. The lines of latitude are labeled in degrees. The equator is 0°. The North Pole is 90°N, while the South Pole is 90°S.

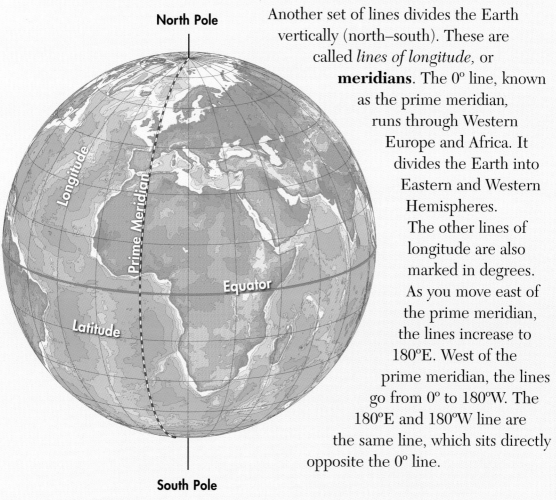

Another set of lines divides the Earth vertically (north–south). These are called *lines of longitude*, or **meridians**. The 0° line, known as the prime meridian, runs through Western Europe and Africa. It divides the Earth into Eastern and Western Hemispheres. The other lines of longitude are also marked in degrees. As you move east of the prime meridian, the lines increase to 180°E. West of the prime meridian, the lines go from 0° to 180°W. The 180°E and 180°W line are the same line, which sits directly opposite the 0° line.

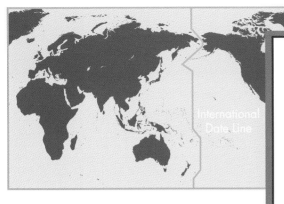

Getting to the Point

The lines of latitude and longitude form a grid across a map. This grid can help you locate places on the map.

The pair of degrees labeling a particular point on a map are called **coordinates**. The degree of latitude is the first number in the pair, followed by the degree of longitude. For example, the general coordinates of Santa Fe, New Mexico, are 35°N, 105°W.

To find Santa Fe on a map, you would find the nearest lines of latitude and longitude and then approximate the distance from those lines. For example, if your map has the 30°N and 60°N lines of latitude marked, 35°N would be slightly above the 30° line. If your globe has lines of longitude marked 90°W and 120°W, then 105°W would be halfway between them. If you find where the 35°N and 105°W lines intersect, Santa Fe should be nearby.

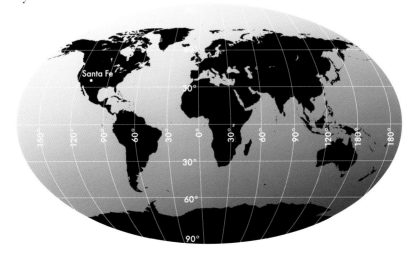

21

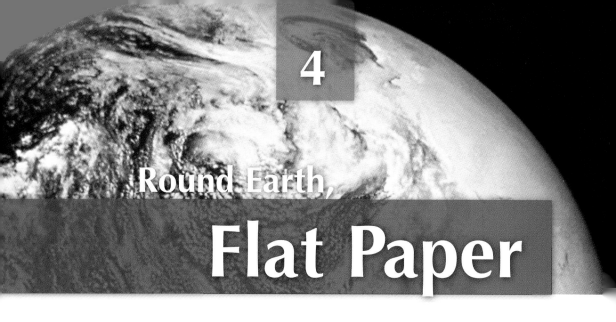

4

Round Earth, Flat Paper

Because the Earth is a sphere, it is most accurately represented on a globe. Unfortunately, globes aren't always the most practical representation. After all, they don't fit very well in your glove compartment or suitcase when you're going on a trip. So mapmakers needed to find ways to transfer a spherical Earth onto a flat piece of paper.

Tracing the Path of Science

Today's globes feature all of the continents and countries of the world. The first globe, however, was quite different from the one in your classroom. It was created by Martin Behaim of Germany. The globe was designed in the style of medieval mapmaking and was covered with legends, descriptions of strange lands, and illustrations of fanciful creatures. It was finished in 1492, the same year that Christopher Columbus discovered America. Columbus hadn't yet returned from his voyage, however, so North and South America were not included on the globe. Behaim's globe was very inaccurate even for his time, but it was the first spherical representation of the world.

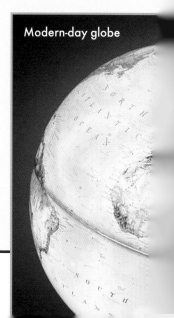

Modern-day globe

The process of putting a three-dimensional image on a two-dimensional surface is known as a **projection**. In mapmaking, there are many types of projections. Each one has advantages and disadvantages, but all are distorted in some way. Four well-known projections are the Mercator, the Mollweide, the Robinson, and the Winkel Tripel.

The Mercator Projection

In 1569, a Dutch cartographer named Gerard Mercator developed a revolutionary map for sea navigators. To do this, he used a cylindrical projection. The projection appears as if a piece of paper were wrapped around a globe like a cylinder and the surface of the globe was projected onto the paper. The paper is then laid out as a flat rectangle. In this type of projection, the lines of latitude and longitude remain perfectly straight, meeting at right angles.

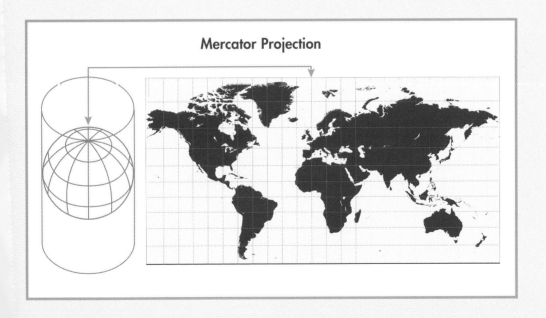

Mercator Projection

The Mercator projection ensures that angles and compass directions remain accurate for navigational use. Sailors can follow a straight line and end up in the same place as if they were following a curved line on a globe. Size, however, is distorted on this projection, especially at the poles. For example, South America appears smaller than Greenland even though it is actually more than eight times larger. Because of these significant distortions, the Mercator projection cannot be used for most purposes.

The Mollweide Projection

Karl B. Mollweide, a German scientist and astronomer, developed the first known pseudocylindrical projection in 1805. A pseudocyclindrical projection is similar to a cylindrical projection, but the top and bottom of the projection point toward the poles. If you can imagine wrapping a piece of paper around a globe and then taping the top and bottom to the poles, you have an idea of how this projection is laid out.

In a Mollweide projection, the Earth is projected as an **ellipse**. Lines of latitude are straight and parallel to the equator, but the lines of longitude are curved around the prime meridian.

The Mollweide projection ensures that individual areas are the correct size in relation to one another. However, there is still some distortion in shape, especially near the edges.

Similar Meanings

The prefix *pseudo-* means "similar to." So a pseudocylindrical projection is similar to a cylindrical projection.

The Robinson Projection

In the early 1960s, the mapmaking company Rand McNally hired geography professor Arthur H. Robinson to develop a new map projection. Robinson used computer simulations to devise another type of pseudocylindrical projection.

The Robinson projection shows the Earth as an oval with a flat top and bottom. The lines of latitude are straight and parallel to the equator, but the lines of longitude curve more like they would on a sphere. The projection evens out all distortions to some degree, but it does not eliminate them.

In 1988, the Robinson projection was adopted by the National Geographic Society as its standard world map.

The Right Map?

The Robinson projection is also called the *orthophanic projection*. *Orthophanic* means "right appearing." Robinson called it this because he felt his map appeared more "right," or correct, than previous ones.

The Winkel Tripel Projection

In 1921, Oswald Winkel created a projection that uses a straight prime meridian and equator but curved lines of latitude and longitude. The projection is called "tripel" (triple) because it reduces the distortion of area, direction, and distance, although it does not eliminate it completely.

For a long time, the Winkel Tripel projection wasn't well known. Then in 1998, the National Geographic Society replaced the Robinson projection with the Winkel Tripel projection because of its better balance of size and shape. This resulted in a great increase in the projection's popularity.

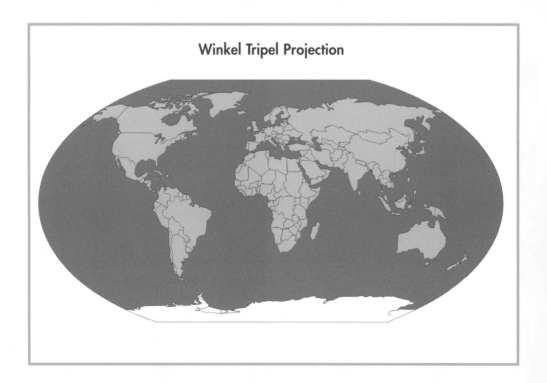

Winkel Tripel Projection

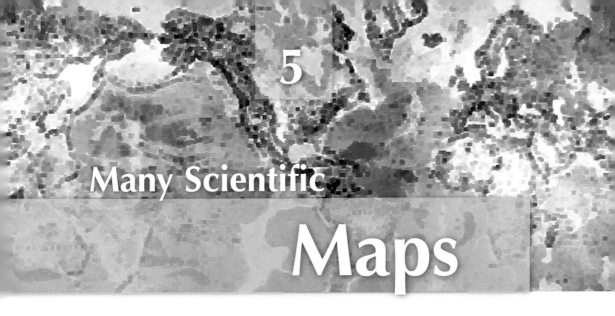

5

Many Scientific Maps

While a lot of maps have a geographical use such as showing the location of places, many types of maps are used in science as well. These maps have a wide variety of purposes.

Land Maps

Several types of maps display natural land features. These include physical, relief, and topographic maps.

A physical map offers a basic view of the land's surface. It identifies landforms and bodies of water. Color is used to highlight differences in land **elevation**.

Relief maps also show land

Physical map of the United States

elevation. In fact, the word *relief* means "a variation in the height of land surfaces." Shaded relief maps use color shading to show the patterns of sunlight and shadows found at different elevations. Very tall mountains, for example, cast dark shadows, while flat plains don't cast shadows at all. Raised relief maps are three-dimensional. Landforms are actually constructed on the surface of the map to show differences in elevation.

Topographic maps show the three-dimensional shape and height of the Earth's features through the use of **contour lines**. Contour lines are lines connecting areas of land with the same elevation. The distance between sets of lines indicates the slope, or slant, of the land. The closer the lines are, the steeper the slope.

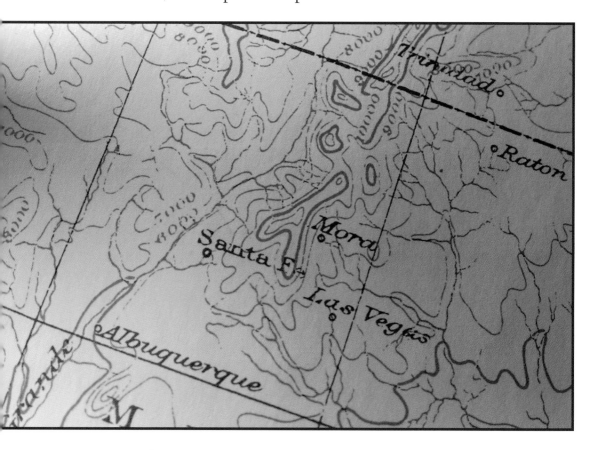

Ocean Floor Maps

About 70 percent of the Earth's surface is covered by ocean. Ocean floor maps show the landforms beneath all of this water. Scientists map basins, ridges, trenches, plateaus, and hot springs. Some maps include the location of underwater **fault lines** and volcanoes. Ocean floor maps also show mountains and islands that begin on the floor but rise out of the water.

Technology Link

How do scientists map the deep, dark ocean floor? They use sonar technology. To do this, scientists place a sonar instrument in the water. The device sends out a pulse of sound energy toward the ocean floor. Sonar equipment measures the time it takes for the sound to hit the floor and bounce back up. This tells how deep the ocean is at that point. A computer plots the depths on a screen. This data can then be used to determine landforms under the water. When sonar measuring is done in a continuous motion, an image of the ocean floor is created. This image can then be used to make a map.

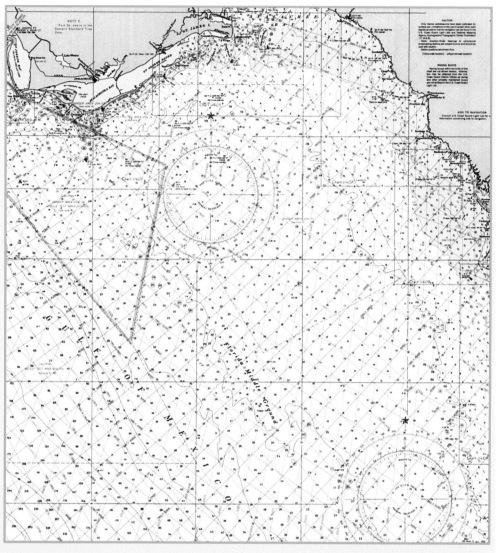

Sea chart of Tampa Bay, Florida

Sea Charts

Sea charts (or nautical charts) are maps of the ocean. These maps outline coasts and islands, provide water depths and currents, and pinpoint important structures such as lighthouses and buoys. Some sea charts also point out dangerous features such as icebergs, underwater mountains, and coral reefs.

Weather Maps

Meteorologists use maps to present current weather conditions and forecast future ones. Different maps can illustrate temperatures, cold and warm fronts, precipitation, air pressure measurements, and storm systems.

Climate maps show which areas of the world have similar climates. Climates are determined by factors such as sunlight, humidity, temperatures, precipitation, and winds. Climate maps generally use different colors to indicate what type of climate an area has. For example, white might represent cold polar regions, while green represents tropical rain forests.

Climate Map of the World

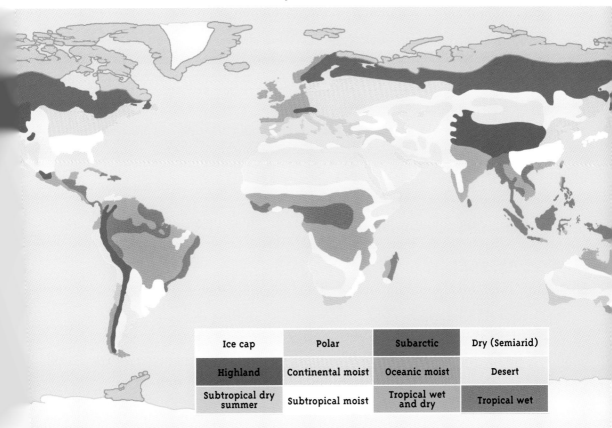

Ice cap	Polar	Subarctic	Dry (Semiarid)
Highland	Continental moist	Oceanic moist	Desert
Subtropical dry summer	Subtropical moist	Tropical wet and dry	Tropical wet

The Geographic Face of the Nation–Land Cover

Geologic Maps

If you want to know what kind of rock lies beneath your feet, a geologic map can help. These maps identify the types of rock found on the Earth's surface (beneath any grass or soil). Geologic maps are useful for finding mineral resources, earthquake faults, and good places for construction or farming.

"Bio" Maps

Biome maps show the location of different biomes around the world. A biome is an environment with unique features. An ocean biome has salt water. A desert biome has a dry climate. A rain forest biome has warm, wet weather year-round. Biome maps mark the areas of the world where these and other biomes can be found.

Biogeographic maps feature the plants and animals that live in certain regions. For example, a map may show where certain types of trees can be found on a continent or where a bird species lives in a state. Scientists use biogeographic maps to study what environmental conditions a specific species needs to survive.

Environmental Maps

Environmental maps can show a variety of environmental factors. Maps that indicate areas at risk for flooding, earthquakes, volcanoes, and other natural disasters are environmental maps. The location of **watersheds** and **aquifers** can be displayed on an environmental map. Environmental maps can also be used to identify landfills, hazardous waste disposal sites, and areas of heavy pollution.

Seismic (earthquake) activity map

6

Mapping Technology

Centuries ago, mapmakers had to rely on observations and ground measurements to create their maps. Today, mapmakers have advanced technology to help them represent the world.

The View from Above

Many mapmakers use aerial photographs as a reliable source of information. Aerial photographs are taken from an airplane as it flies above the Earth in a straight line. These pictures can then be used to make accurate maps of the land.

Satellites are also used to collect images of the Earth. A satellite is a spacecraft that orbits the Earth gathering information with special sensors and cameras. This data is sent to a computer where it is converted into an image that mapmakers can use.

MapQuest

Have you ever used MapQuest to figure out the best way to get somewhere? MapQuest is an online mapping program that provides users with a map of a location and directions to get there. It works through the use of computer **servers** that process information on a given location and translate the data into a map and directions.

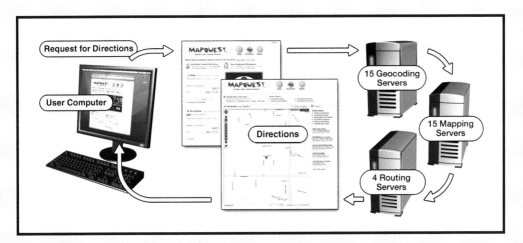

Global Positioning Systems

Global Positioning Systems (GPS) are like personal maps that show you where you are at all times. This technology was first created for military purposes but is now available to the general public. It is often used in cars, planes, and ships. It is also helpful for mapmakers surveying an area of land. GPS works through the use of satellites and receivers. A GPS receiver evaluates radio signals that bounce off satellites orbiting the Earth. The receiver determines its location based on the length of these signals.

Handheld GPS device

35

Geographic Information Systems

Imagine you're planning a new development in your city. To do this, you'll need to know the layout of the land, including roadways, buildings, water sources, pipelines, and other information. Instead of using a separate map for each factor, you could use a geographic information system, or GIS.

A GIS is a computerized map system that combines different information about an area and displays it for easy use. Each computer command can bring up a new set of data that can be combined with other sets in order to see "the whole picture." With GIS, an entire system of maps is right at your fingertips.

❖ ❖ ❖ ❖ ❖

As the world changes, so does the job of the mapmaker. Each generation uses new technology to map its view of the world.

Internet Connections and Related Reading for Maps

http://www.nationalgeographic.com/homework/
Find out more about maps and projections, access an online atlas, and make your own customized maps at this National Geographic site for students. (Visit the "maps/geography" section.)

http://www.msnucleus.org/membership/html/jh/earth/mapstype/index.html
Mini-lessons and activities provide an overview of different types of maps.

http://www.enchantedlearning.com/geography/mapreading/
Practice your map reading skills with the printable activities at this site.

http://www.enchantedlearning.com/geography/glossary/projections.shtml
Check out this student-friendly introduction to map projections and related concepts such as latitude and longitude.

DK Student Atlas by DK editors. This updated edition of DK's revolutionary student atlas teaches essential map skills while touching on the latest changes and developments in climate, conservation, land use, industry, population, and much more. Dorling Kindersley, 2004. ISBN 0-7566-0338-2. [IL 5–8] (2716506 HB)

National Geographic Student Atlas of the World by National Geographic editors. This new edition of the award-winning original features more pages, full-color photographs, illustrations and satellite images, charts, graphs, and facts boxes. National Geographic, 2005. ISBN 0-7922-7178-5. [IL 7–12] (2397206 HB)

National Geographic World Atlas for Young Explorers by National Geographic editors. The large-format maps, created by expert cartographers, are accompanied by vivid text to make an exciting connection between maps and the real world. National Geographic, 2003. ISBN 0-7922-2879-0. [IL 3–7] (3405506 HB)

•RL = Reading Level
•IL = Interest Level
Perfection Learning's catalog numbers are included for your ordering convenience.
HB indicates hardback.

Glossary

aquifer   (AHK wuh fer) layer of rock that contains groundwater used to supply wells and springs

atlas   (AT luhs) book containing maps and statistics of regions

biome   (BEYE ohm) environment with unique features, such as the grasslands, rain forests, and deserts

cartography   (kar TAHG ruh fee) science, art, or job of making maps

climate   (KLEYE mit) usual weather in an area over a period of time

compass rose   (KUHM puhs rohz) diagram on a map that shows the directions

contour line   (KAHN toor leyen) line on a map that connects land at the same elevation

coordinate   (koh OR duh nuht) one of a pair of numbers that identifies the latitude or longitude of a specific location

cosmography   (kahz MAH gruh fee) study of mapping the world or universe

elevation   (el uh VAY shuhn) height above sea level

ellipse   (ee LIPS) shape resembling a stretched-out circle with slightly longer, flatter sides

fault line   (fawlt leyen) line or crack on the Earth's surface where layers of rock have broken apart and earthquakes may occur

key   (kee) explanation of the symbols and colors on a map; legend

latitude   (LAT uh tood) imaginary line circling the globe horizontally

legend	(LEDJ uhnd) explanation of the symbols and colors on a map; key
longitude	(LAHN juh tood) imaginary line circling the globe vertically; meridian
map	(map) visual representation of features found on all or part of a planet's surface
meridian	(muh RID ee uhn) imaginary line circling the globe vertically; line of longitude
projection	(pruh JEK shuhn) image or picture transferred onto a surface
satellite	(SAT uh leyet) object that orbits the Earth to collect images and information
scale	(skayl) ratio that tells the relationship between the distance on a map and the distance in real life
server	(SERV er) computer that stores programs and data files accessed by other computers in a network; file server
watershed	(WAW ter shed) area of land drained by a river

Index

aerial photography, 34
atlases, 13
Behaim, Martin, 22
cartography, 6
compass rose, 15
compasses, 12, 15, 16–17
contour lines, 28
coordinates, 21
cosmography, 11
elevation, 27, 28
geographic information systems, 36
Global Positioning Systems, 35
globes, 22
keys/legends, 19
large-scale maps, 18
lines of latitude, 20, 21
lines of longitude (meridians), 20, 21
map projections, 23–26
    Mercator, 23–24
    Mollweide, 24
    Robinson, 25
    Winkel Tripel, 26
MapQuest, 35
maps
    definition, 5
    history, 7–13

Mercator, Gerard, 23
Mollweide, Karl B., 24
Munster, Sebastian, 11
Ortelius, Abraham, 13
Ptolemy, 9–10, 12
Robinson, Arthur H., 25
satellite imaging, 34
scales, 18
small-scale maps, 18
types of maps
    biogeographic maps, 33
    biome maps, 32
    climate maps, 5, 31
    environmental maps, 33
    geologic maps, 32
    ocean floor maps, 5, 28, 29
    physical maps, 27
    portolan maps (sea charts), 12, 30
    relief maps, 27
    topographic maps, 28
    weather maps, 31
Winkel, Oswald, 26